The Cookbook to Your Better Chicken Piccata

Enjoy Delicious Chicken Piccata Recipes

BY

Jayden Dixon

Copyright 2022 Jayden Dixon

Copyright Notes

Fortunately, all of my readers are really nice people, and I don't have to worry too much about asking everyone to please refrain from sharing my work with others because then I don't get credit for it. Either way, I still like to add a little section in all of my books specifying what is NOT allowed so you can avoid copyright infringements.

Do not sell, re-publish, distribute, or make any print or electronic reproductions of this book in parts or as a whole unless you have express written consent from my team or me. We're so strict about it because we value our work and want to receive proper credit for all the time we put into this book.

Anyway, I know this isn't going to be an issue…I just had to put it out there just in case. With that out of the way, we can finally start cooking, so let's go!

Table of Contents

Introduction 5

1. Chicken Piccata in Lime Sauce 7

2. Chicken Piccata in White Sauce 10

3. Chicken Piccata Spaghetti 13

4. Cheesy Chicken Lime Piccata 16

5. Chicken Piccata with Green Beans 19

6. Crispy Chicken piccata 22

7. Chicken Piccata with Artichokes and Spinach 24

8. Spicy Chicken Piccata Fettuccine 27

9. Creamy Chicken Piccata Noodles 30

10. Coriander Flavored Chicken Piccata 32

11. Chicken Piccata with Mushroom and Noodles 34

12. Crispy Chicken Piccata with Macaroni Pasta 37

13. Chicken Piccata Green Bean Pasta 40

14. Pasta with Chicken Piccata and Asparagus 43

15. Chicken Piccata Pizza 46

16. Mint Lime Chicken Piccata 49

17. Creamy Mushroom White Sauce Chicken Piccata 51

18. Chicken piccata in Curry Flavor 54

19. Zesty Chicken Piccata Pasta 57

20. Chicken Piccata Bowtie Pasta 60

21. Chicken Piccata with Veggies and Noodles 63

22. Chicken Piccata with Arugula Salad 66

23. Garlic Fig Flavored Chicken Piccata 69

24. Chicken Piccata with Roasted Potatoes 72

25. Chicken Piccata with Mashed Potatoes 75

26. Chicken Piccata with Spaghetti 78

27. Creamy Chicken Piccata Soup 80

28. Chicken Piccata Penne Pasta 83

29. Chicken Piccata Veg Soup 86

30. Artichoke Spinach Chicken Piccata 89

Conclusion 92

Author's Afterthoughts 93

About the Author 94

Introduction

The chicken piccata recipe is one of those dishes that is ready in minutes, but it has massive flavor profiles.

The history of chicken piccata goes back to 1930! Surprisingly it was invented in the USA by Italian immigrants. They initially prepared it with veal instead of chicken. At that time, veal was much cheaper than the chicken itself. Although now, the story is quite different. Chicken is readily available and affordable by every community around the world now.

The lime slices and lime juice are also an important element of the dish. You cannot skip it. Even if you decide to skin lime slices, you need to use lime juice to get the real flavor of chicken piccata. Traditionally it is made with lime slices, lime juice, butter, a little bit of spices, chicken, herbs, and capers. Capers are important and you cannot skip it either in the recipe.

Then comes the work of fusion where you can make chicken piccata pasta, chicken piccata soup, chicken piccata pizza or even chicken piccata stir fry.

The choice is yours how far you want to drag the recipe and how creative you want to be in the kitchen.

In the book, you will find 30 delicious and different chicken piccata recipes that I am sure you will love.

1. Chicken Piccata in Lime Sauce

This is a crispy chicken piccata recipe with zesty lime brine.

Preparation Time: 5 minutes

Cooking Time: 20 minutes

Serves: 6

Ingredients:

- 6 chicken breasts
- 2 tbsp lime juice
- 1 lime, sliced thinly
- 1 can (4 oz) capers in brine
- 2 tbsp parsley, chopped
- 1/2 cup all-purpose flour
- 1 tsp paprika
- 1 tsp white pepper
- Salt to taste
- 2 tbsp butter

Instructions:

Remove the skin of the chicken breasts.

Coat the chicken in salt, white pepper and paprika.

Coat them generously in all-purpose flour.

In a pan, add half the butter.

Fry the chicken pieces until crispy from both sides.

Transfer the chicken pieces on a plate.

In the same pan, add the rest of the butter.

Add the lime juice, and capers.

Toss for 4 minutes. Add the fried chicken pieces.

Add lime slices, and cover with a lid.

Cook for 3 minutes. Top with parsley and serve.

2. Chicken Piccata in White Sauce

The delicious white sauce chicken piccata recipe is amazing.

Preparation Time: 5 minutes

Cooking Time: 25 minutes

Serves: 4

Ingredients:

- 4 chicken breasts, skinless
- 1 lime, cut into wedges
- 1/2 can (4 oz) capers, in brine
- 4 tbsp all-purpose flour
- 3 tbsp breadcrumbs
- 6 tbsp butter
- 1 tsp chives, minced
- 1/2 cup cheddar cheese, grated
- 1/2 cup milk
- Salt and pepper
- 1 tsp paprika
- 1 tsp garlic powder

Instructions:

In a large skillet, melt 2 tbsp of the butter.

Coat the chicken in salt, pepper and garlic powder.

Combine the breadcrumbs with paprika.

Generously coat the chicken pieces in the breadcrumb mix.

Fry them in the butter until they are golden in color.

Take the chicken pieces out on a plate.

In the same skillet, add the rest of the butter.

Add the flour and toss on low flame for 2 minutes.

Add the milk slowly and stir for 1 minute.

Add the cheddar cheese and stir for 2 minutes.

Add the lime slices, capers and seasoning.

Return the chicken pieces and cook for 4 minutes.

Add the chives on top and serve hot.

Add the cheese and parsley and serve hot.

3. Chicken Piccata Spaghetti

Have you ever tried something like this before? Chicken piccata chopped into smaller bits with cherry tomato spaghetti?

Preparation Time: 10 minutes

Cooking Time: 30 minutes

Serves: 4

Ingredients:

- 1 cup spaghetti
- 1/2 cup cherry tomatoes
- 4 chicken breasts
- 4 tbsp flour
- 1/2 can (2 oz) capers, in brine
- 1 lime, sliced thinly
- 10 olives, pitted, chopped
- 2 tbsp butter
- 2 tbsp olive oil
- 2 tbsp scallions, chopped
- Salt and pepper to taste
- 1 tsp red chili powder
- 1 tsp paprika
- 2 tbsp chives, chopped
- 4 tbsp tomato sauce
- 1 tsp rosemary

Instructions:

Boil the spaghetti in a pot with salted water.

Combine the paprika, salt, and pepper with flour.

Sprinkle the salt, pepper and rosemary onto the chicken breasts.

Coat them in flour mix.

In a pan, melt the butter, fry the chicken breasts for 3 minutes per side.

Take them out on a plate. Let it rest for 5 minutes.

Chop the chicken into smaller cubes.

In a large skillet, add the olive oil.

Toss the cherry tomatoes, olives, scallions and boiled spaghetti for 5 minutes.

Add seasoning and tomato sauce. Add lime slices, capers, red chili powder, chives, paprika, and red chili powder. Cook for 2 minutes and return the chicken to the skillet.

Cook for another 2 minutes. Serve hot.

4. Cheesy Chicken Lime Piccata

Here is another simple chicken piccata recipe with a cheesy and creamy twist to it.

Preparation Time: 5 minutes

Cooking Time: 25 minutes

Serves: 4

Ingredients:

- 4 chicken breasts
- 1/2 can (2 oz) capers, in brine
- 1/2 cup cheddar cheese, grated
- 4 tbsp butter
- 2 tbsp lime juice
- 1 lime, chopped roughly
- 2 tbsp parsley, minced
- 1 tsp oregano
- 1 tsp garlic powder
- Salt and pepper

Instructions:

Sprinkle the garlic, salt, pepper onto the chicken pieces.

In a pan, melt 1 tbsp of the butter.

Fry the chicken pieces until golden brown from both sides.

Transfer them to a plate.

Add the rest of the butter to the pan.

Add the capers and toss for 2 minutes.

Add the oregano, some salt, lime juice, pepper and toss for 1 minute.

Add the chicken again and top with the cheese.

Cook for 2 minutes. Add the lime pieces and parsley. Serve.

5. Chicken Piccata with Green Beans

Are you tired of eating the same chicken piccata? Then try this one, it has green beans and the spicy kick to the chicken is very appealing for the spice lovers.

Preparation Time: 5 minutes

Cooking Time: 30 minutes

Serves: 5

Ingredients:

- 5 chicken thighs, boneless
- 2 limes, cut into half-moon shape slices
- 2 cups green beans, trimmed
- 1 tsp paprika
- 1 tsp red chili powder
- 1 tsp cayenne
- 1 can (4 oz) capers, in brine
- 4 tbsp butter
- 1 tsp oregano
- 1 tsp garlic powder
- Salt and pepper

Instructions:

Coat the chicken thighs using cayenne, salt, garlic and pepper.

In a large skillet, melt 1 tbsp of the butter.

Fry the chicken pieces until they are brown from both sides.

Take them off the heat.

In the same skillet, add the rest of the butter.

Add the green beans. Add red chili powder, paprika, capers, oregano and seasonings.

Cook for 5 minutes. Add the chicken again and the lime slices.

Cook for 3 minutes. Serve.

6. Crispy Chicken piccata

This is a very simple chicken piccata recipe with basic ingredients on, but the taste is super delicious.

Preparation Time: 5 minutes

Cooking Time: 15 minutes

Serves: 1

Ingredients:

- 1 chicken breast
- 2 tbsp breadcrumbs
- 1 lime, cut into thin slices
- 1/4 can (1 oz) capers, in brine
- 2 tsp parsley, chopped
- 2 tbsp butter
- Salt and pepper
- 1 tsp garlic powder

Instructions:

Coat the chicken in salt, pepper and garlic powder.

Coat it in breadcrumbs.

In a pan, add 1 tsp of butter and fry the chicken until crispy.

Transfer to a plate.

In the same pan, add the rest of the butter.

Add the capers and toss for 2 minutes.

Add lime slices, parsley, and chicken again.

Toss for 3 minutes. Serve.

7. Chicken Piccata with Artichokes and Spinach

Here is a different take on the classic chicken piccata recipe. You will find the spinach and artichoke in it very refreshing.

Preparation Time: 5 minutes

Cooking Time: 30 minutes

Serves: 3

Ingredients:

- 3 chicken breasts
- 1 lime, cut into wedges
- 1 cup spinach, chopped
- 1/2 cup artichoke hearts, cleaned, sliced
- 1/2 can (2 oz) capers, in brine
- 1 cup chicken stock
- 1 tsp red chili powder
- 1 tsp garlic powder
- 3 tbsp butter
- 2 tbsp breadcrumbs
- 2 tbsp lime juice
- Salt and pepper

Instructions:

Coat the chicken in garlic, salt, pepper and breadcrumbs.

In a skillet, add 1 tbsp of the butter and fry the chicken breasts until they are golden brown.

Take them out on a plate.

In the skillet, add the rest of the butter.

Fry the artichoke, capers for 2 minutes.

Add the lime juice, seasoning, red chili powder, and chicken stock.

Simmer for 5 minutes. Add the chicken and spinach.

Cook for 3 minutes. Add the lime wedges and serve.

8. Spicy Chicken Piccata Fettuccine

If you enjoy eating fettuccine then you will love this chicken piccata version of it

Preparation Time: 5 minutes

Cooking Time: 20 minutes

Serves: 43

Ingredients:

- 3 chicken breasts
- 2 cups fettuccine
- 1/2 cup parmesan cheese, grated
- 3 tbsp breadcrumbs
- 2 tbsp chives, chopped
- 1 tbsp parsley, chopped
- 1 tbsp olive oil
- 2 tbsp butter
- Salt to taste
- 1 tsp paprika
- 1 tsp black pepper
- 1 tsp garlic powder
- 1 tsp lime juice

Instructions:

Boil the fettuccine in water for 6 minutes.

Drain them and keep aside for now.

Coat the chicken breasts in salt, garlic, pepper, and lime juice.

Coat them in breadcrumbs.

In a large skillet, add half the butter.

Fry the chicken until brown. Take them out of a plate.

In the skillet, add the remaining butter.

Add the fettuccine and toss for 2 minutes.

Add salt, pepper, olive oil, chives, parsley, and paprika.

Return the chicken to the skillet.

Add the cheese and cook for 3 minutes. Serve hot.

9. Creamy Chicken Piccata Noodles

The creaminess of the chicken is mind blowing. It is complementary to the noodles. The capers on top of also delicious with the noodles.

Preparation Time: 5 minutes

Cooking Time: 20 minutes

Serves: 2

Ingredients:

- 2 chicken breasts, halved
- 1/2 can (2 oz) capers, in brine
- 1/2 cup cheddar cheese, grated
- 1 cup noodles
- 1/2 cup coconut milk
- 1 tbsp lime juice
- 1 tsp oregano
- 1 tbsp parsley, chopped
- 1 tsp garlic powder
- 1 tbsp butter
- Salt and black pepper

Instructions:

Boil the noodles in salted water for 6 minutes.

Drain and add to a serving plate.

Coat the chicken in salt, oregano, garlic, and pepper.

In a pan, add the chicken with butter and cook until golden.

Pour in the coconut milk, capers, parsley, and seasonings.

Cook for 5 minutes. Add the cheddar cheese.

Cook for 2 minutes. Add on top of the noodles. Serve.

10. Coriander Flavored Chicken Piccata

This chicken piccata recipe is packed with coriander flavors. The caper in the recipe also adds more taste to the chicken.

Preparation Time: 5 minutes

Cooking Time: 20 minutes

Serves: 4

Ingredients:

- 4 chicken breasts
- 1 can (4 oz) capers, in brine
- 4 tbsp coriander, chopped
- 4 tbsp butter
- 2 tbsp lime juice
- 4 tbsp flour
- 1 tsp garlic powder
- 1 tsp ginger powder
- Salt and pepper

Instructions:

Coat the chicken in salt, pepper, flour, and garlic.

In a large pan, add 2 tbsp butter.

fry the chicken breasts until they are golden in color.

Transfer the chicken pieces on a plate.

Onto the same pan, add the rest of the butter.

Add the capers and cook for 2 minutes.

Add the coriander, lime juice and ginger.

Add some seasoning. Return the chicken piece.

Cook for 4 minutes. Serve hot.

11. Chicken Piccata with Mushroom and Noodles

Try this chicken piccata recipe with mushrooms and capers. The taste of rosemary and oregano is evident in the recipe. The rice noodles also taste amazing.

Preparation Time: 5 minutes

Cooking Time: 30 minutes

Serves: 2

Ingredients:

- 2 chicken breasts, halved
- 1 cup rice noodles
- 2 tsp all-purpose flour
- 1/2 cup mushrooms, sliced
- 1/2 can (2 oz) capers, in brine
- 4 tbsp butter
- 1 tsp oregano
- 1 tsp rosemary
- 1 tsp cayenne
- Salt and pepper

Instructions:

Coat the chicken pieces in salt, pepper, and cayenne.

Coat it in all-purpose flour as well.

In a pan, melt 1 tbsp of the butter.

Fry the chicken until golden brown.

Transfer the chicken on a plate.

Add the remaining butter. Add the mushroom.

Stir for 2 minutes. Add capers, oregano, seasoning and rosemary.

Toss for 1 minute. Return the chicken.

Cook for 4 minutes. Boil the rice noodles in salted water.

Add the chicken mushroom mix on top of the noodles. Serve.

12. Crispy Chicken Piccata with Macaroni Pasta

The delicious macaroni pasta with crispy and herb chicken piccata is delicious.

Preparation Time: 5 minutes

Cooking Time: 25 minutes

Serves: 2

Ingredients:

- 2 chicken thighs, boneless
- 2 tbsp breadcrumbs
- 1 tsp oregano
- 1 tsp garlic powder
- 1 1/2 cups macaroni pasta
- 1/2 cup spinach
- 2 tbsp basil leaves, chopped
- 1 tsp ginger powder
- Salt and pepper
- 1 tsp smoked paprika
- 1/2 cup parmesan cheese, grated
- 2 tbsp butter

Instructions:

Coat the chicken thighs in salt, pepper, garlic and paprika.

Coat them in breadcrumbs as well.

In a pan, add 1 tbsp of butter.

Fry the chicken pieces until crispy.

Add them to a plate.

In the same pan, melt the rest of the butter.

Add the boiled macaroni.

Add spinach, basil, ginger, oregano, seasoning and cook for 5 minutes.

Add cheese and cook for 2 minutes.

Add the chicken pieces on top and serve hot.

13. Chicken Piccata Green Bean Pasta

Here is a twist on chicken piccata and pasta, I bet you will love the combination.

Preparation Time: 10 minutes

Cooking Time: 20 minutes

Serves: 4

Ingredients:

- 2 cups pasta of your choice
- 2 chicken breasts, cut into small cubes
- 2 tbsp flour
- 1 lime, cut into wedges
- 2 tbsp lime juice
- 1 cup green beans, diced roughly
- 1 onion, chopped
- 1 tsp oregano
- 1 tsp rosemary
- 1 tsp smoked paprika
- 1 tsp ginger powder
- Salt and pepper
- 1 tsp parsley, chopped
- 3 tbsp butter
- 1/2 can (2 oz) capers, in brine

Instructions:

Boil the pasta in water for 6 minutes.

Drain well and keep aside for now.

Coat the chicken in salt, pepper, paprika and flour.

In a large skillet, fry the chicken pieces with 1 tbsp butter, until golden in color.

Transfer them to a plate.

Add the remaining butter to the skillet.

Fry the onion for 1 minute.

Add the capers, green beans. Add seasoning, rosemary, oregano, ginger and cook for 2 minutes.

Add the boiled pasta, lime juice and chicken pieces.

Cook for 5 minutes. Add parsley and lime wedges. Serve.

14. Pasta with Chicken Piccata and Asparagus

This recipe is the perfect balance of protein and crab. Also, a perfect balance of veggie, meat and gluten.

Preparation Time: 5 minutes

Cooking Time: 25 minutes

Serves: 2

Ingredients:

- 2 chicken thighs, boneless
- 1 tbsp breadcrumbs
- 1/2 cup asparagus
- 1 cup pasta of your choice
- 1/4 can (1 oz) capers, in brine
- 2 tbsp butter
- 2 tbsp lime juice
- 1 tbsp olive oil
- Salt and pepper
- 2 tbsp lemon juice
- 1 tsp garlic powder

Instructions:

Coat the chicken in seasoning, garlic and breadcrumbs.

Boil the pasta in water for 6 minutes.

Drain the pasta and keep aside.

In a pan, add half of the butter.

Fry the chicken thighs until they are golden brown.

Transfer the chicken thighs on the plate.

Add the rest of the butter to the pan.

Add the asparagus and toss for 3 minutes with seasoning.

Add the capers in the pan, add lime juice.

Return the chicken thighs and toss for 3 minutes.

Serve the pasta with chicken thighs and asparagus.

15. Chicken Piccata Pizza

Who would have thought of having chicken piccata, but apparently it is delicious.

Preparation Time: 2 hours

Cooking Time: 30 minutes

Serves: 6

Ingredients:

- 2 cups all-purpose flour
- 2/3 cup warm milk
- 1 tsp garlic powder
- 2 tsp dry active yeast
- 4 chicken breasts
- 2 tsp sugar
- 4 tbsp breadcrumbs
- 10 black olives, sliced
- 2 tbsp basil, chopped
- 1 cup cheddar cheese, grated
- 4 tbsp tomato sauce
- 4 tbsp pomegranate seeds
- 1 tsp oregano
- 2 tbsp butter
- Salt and pepper
- 1 tbsp olive oil
- 1 tsp smoked paprika

Instructions:

In a mixing bowl, combine the warm milk with sugar.

Add the active yeast.

Stir well and keep aside with the lid on for 10 minutes.

Add the flour, olive oil, garlic powder and salt.

Knead well for 10 minutes. Keep aside with a lid on for another 2 hours.

Meanwhile, prepare the chicken. Coat it in breadcrumbs, salt, pepper, oregano, and paprika.

In a pan, fry the chicken with butter until golden brown.

Take off the heat. Chop it finely.

Now, grease a pizza pan.

Knead the dough again and add to the pizza pan.

Spread the tomato sauce. Add the chopped chicken.

Add basil, cheese, olives, seasoning, and bake for 20 minutes.

Serve with pomegranate seeds on top.

16. Mint Lime Chicken Piccata

The delicious recipe with mint and lime flavored to make the chicken piccata outstanding.

Preparation Time: 5 minutes

Cooking Time: 20 minutes

Serves: 4

Ingredients:

- 4 chicken breasts, boneless, halved
- 2 tbsp all-purpose flour
- 1 tsp cayenne
- 3 tbsp mint leaves
- 1/2 can (2 oz) capers, in brine
- 1 tsp oregano
- 1 tsp garlic powder
- Salt and pepper
- 1 lime, sliced
- 2 tbsp lime juice
- 2 tbsp butter

Instructions:

Coat the chicken pieces in all-purpose flour, salt, pepper, cayenne, garlic and let it sit for 5 minutes.

In a skillet, add half the butter.

Fry the chicken pieces until golden brown.

Add the rest of the butter, add capers, mint leaves and lime slices.

Add more seasoning and oregano.

Cook for 3 minutes. Add lime juice and cook for 2 minutes. Serve hot.

17. Creamy Mushroom White Sauce Chicken Piccata

If you enjoy anything with white sauce, you will love this chicken piccata combo with white sauce. The mushrooms in it are an added plus for the recipe!

Preparation Time: 5 minutes

Cooking Time: 30 minutes

Serves: 2

Ingredients:

- 2 chicken breasts
- 2 bacon strips
- 6 tbsp butter
- 1 tbsp olive oil
- 1 cup milk
- 2 tbsp parsley, chopped
- 4 tbsp flour
- 2 tbsp breadcrumbs
- 1/2 cup cheddar cheese, shredded
- 1 tsp paprika
- 1/2 can (2 oz) capers, in brine
- 1 tsp white pepper
- 1 tsp oregano
- Salt to taste

Instructions:

Coat the chicken pieces in breadcrumbs, salt, and paprika and let it sit for 5 minutes.

In a skillet, add the oil. Fry the chicken until golden brown.

Transfer to a plate.

In a large pot, add the butter.

Fry the flour for 2 minutes on low flame.

Add the milk and stir for 2 minutes.

Add cheddar, seasoning, white pepper, oregano, and cook for 3 minutes.

Add capers, parsley, chicken and cook for 5 minutes.

Fry the bacon until crispy. Crumble it and add on top of the chicken. Serve.

18. Chicken piccata in Curry Flavor

This is a curried version of the chicken piccata recipe. The gravy of the curry is finger-licking good in the recipe.

Preparation Time: 5 minutes

Cooking Time: 25 minutes

Serves: 4

Ingredients:

- 4 chicken breasts
- 1 lime, sliced
- 1/2 can (2 oz) capers, in brine
- 1 tsp garlic powder
- 1 tsp ginger powder
- 1 tsp cayenne
- 1 tsp cumin
- 1 tsp coriander
- Salt and white pepper
- 2 tbsp parsley, minced
- 1/2 cup chicken broth
- 2 tbsp flour
- 2 tbsp butter

Instructions:

Coat the chicken pieces in flour, garlic, salt, and pepper.

In a pan, add 1 tsp of butter.

Fry the chicken pieces until golden.

Transfer the chicken pieces on a plate.

In the same pan, add the butter.

Add garlic, ginger, cayenne, cumin, coriander, salt and 2 tsp of chicken broth.

Cook for 3 minutes. Add the rest of the chicken broth.

Cook for 4 minutes. Add the chicken again.

Add parsley, lime slices and capers.

Cook for 5 minutes. Serve hot.

19. Zesty Chicken Piccata Pasta

Here is a different take on the classic chicken piccata and pasta. The rosemary flavor is strong in this recipe.

Preparation Time: 5 minutes

Cooking Time: 20 minutes

Serves: 4

Ingredients:

- 2 cups pasta
- 1 tbsp rosemary, minced
- 2 chicken breasts, cut into small cubes
- 1 tsp coriander, minced
- 1 tsp oregano
- 2 tbsp lime juice
- 1 tsp cayenne
- 2 tbsp shallots, chopped
- Salt and pepper
- 1/2 cup cheddar cheese, grated
- 1 tbsp butter
- 2 tbsp breadcrumbs
- 1 tbsp oil

Instructions:

Boil the pasta in water for 6 minutes.

Drain them and keep aside.

Coat the chicken cubes in salt, breadcrumbs, pepper and cayenne.

In a pan, add the butter. Fry the chicken cubes until golden brown.

Transfer the chicken in kitchen tissue.

In a wok, add the oil. Fry the shallots for 2 minutes.

Add the pasta, chicken cubes, seasoning, oregano, and rosemary.

Stir for 2 minutes. Add cheddar and lime juice.

Cook for 1 minute. Serve with coriander on top.

20. Chicken Piccata Bowtie Pasta

The creamy and juicy flavor of the chicken piccata pasta is overwhelming in a good way!

Preparation Time: 5 minutes

Cooking Time: 25 minutes

Serves: 4

Ingredients:

- 2 chicken thighs, boneless
- 2 tbsp breadcrumbs
- 2 cups bowtie pasta
- 1 tsp garlic powder
- 1 tsp paprika
- 2 tbsp basil, minced
- 1/3 cup tomato sauce
- 1/4 cup shallots, chopped
- 1 tbsp oil
- 1 tbsp butter
- Salt and pepper
- 1/2 cup parmesan cheese, grated
- 1/2 cup cheddar cheese, grated

Instructions:

Boil the pasta for 6 minutes. Drain well.

Coat the chicken thighs in breadcrumbs, salt and pepper.

In a pan, add the butter. Fry the chicken thighs until golden.

Add to a kitchen tissue.

In a wok, add the oil. Fry the shallot for 1 minute.

Chop the chicken thighs finely.

Add to the wok. Add the boiled bowtie pasta.

Add seasoning, tomato sauce, paprika, garlic, and cook for 3 minutes.

Add the cheddar and parmesan. Cook for 3 minutes. Serve with basil on top.

21. Chicken Piccata with Veggies and Noodles

The combination of chicken piccata and noodles is quite interesting. It complements each other and adding the veggies like zucchini and mushroom further enhances the entire recipe here.

Preparation Time: 5 minutes

Cooking Time: 30 minutes

Serves: 2

Ingredients:

- 1 cup noodles
- 2 chicken breasts
- 1 zucchini, sliced
- 1/3 cup mushrooms, sliced
- 2 tbsp breadcrumbs
- 1 tsp paprika
- Salt and pepper to taste
- 1 tsp garlic powder
- 1 tsp oregano
- 2 tbsp butter

Instructions:

Boil the noodles in salted water for 6 minutes.

Drain the noodles and keep aside.

Coat the breadcrumbs, salt, garlic and pepper.

In a pan, add half the butter.

Fry the chicken until golden brown.

Transfer the chicken on a plate.

In the same pan, add the rest of the butter.

Fry the mushroom for 1 minute.

Add the zucchini slices. Add seasoning, paprika, and oregano.

Cook for 3 minutes. Assemble the noodles, chicken and zucchini mix.

Serve hot.

22. Chicken Piccata with Arugula Salad

The combo of chicken piccata with arugula cherry tomato salad is quite interesting.

Preparation Time: 5 minutes

Cooking Time: 20 minutes

Serves: 2

Ingredients:

- 2 chicken breasts
- 1 lime, sliced
- 1/2 can (2 oz) capers, in brine
- 1 cup arugula
- 1/2 cup cherry tomatoes, halved
- 1 tsp cayenne
- 1 tbsp olive oil
- 2 tbsp flour
- 1 tsp garlic powder
- 3 tbsp butter
- 1 tbsp lime juice
- 2 tbsp parsley, minced
- Salt and pepper to taste

Instructions:

Combine the arugula, cherry tomatoes, olive oil, salt and pepper.

Toss well and add to a serving plate.

Coat the chicken breasts in flour, salt, and cayenne.

In a pan, add 1 tbsp of butter. Fry the chicken until brown.

Transfer to a plate. In the pan, add 2 tbsp of butter.

Add capers, parsley, cayenne, garlic and seasoning.

Add the lime juice, lime slices and chicken. Cook for 5 minutes.

Assemble everything and serve.

23. Garlic Fig Flavored Chicken Piccata

The fig adds a slight sweetness to the recipe and the zestiness from the lime balances out the entire recipe.

Preparation Time: 5 minutes

Cooking Time: 20 minutes

Serves: 4

Ingredients:

- 4 chicken breasts
- 1 lime, sliced
- 2 tbsp lime juice
- 2 tbsp parsley, chopped
- 1/2 can (2 oz) capers, in brine
- 1/2 cup fig, chopped
- 3 garlic cloves, halved
- 1 tsp rosemary
- 4 tbsp breadcrumbs
- 1 tsp red chili powder
- 1 tbsp oil
- 2 tbsp butter
- Salt and white pepper to taste

Instructions:

Coat the chicken breast in breadcrumbs, salt, white pepper and let it sit for 5 minutes.

In a pan, add the oil.

Fry the chicken breasts for 3 minutes per side.

Take them off the heat.

In the same pan, melt the butter.

Add the garlic and cook until golden.

Add fig, capers, seasoning, rosemary and lime juice.

Add red chili powder, lime slices and cook for 2 minutes.

Add the chicken again. Add parsley and cook for 3 minutes. Serve hot.

24. Chicken Piccata with Roasted Potatoes

The chicken piccata goes pretty well with roasted potatoes. The arugula on top adds subtle freshness to the recipe.

Preparation Time: 5 minutes

Cooking Time: 30 minutes

Serves: 1

Ingredients:

- 1 chicken breast
- 1/2 cup arugula
- 1/4 can (2 oz) capers, in brine
- 1/2 cup potatoes, cut into wedges
- 1/3 tsp garlic powder
- 1/3 tsp rosemary
- 1 tbsp parsley, chopped
- 1 tbsp butter
- 1 tbsp lime juice
- 1 tsp oil
- 1 tbsp breadcrumbs
- Salt and pepper

Instructions:

Coat the chicken breast in breadcrumbs, salt and pepper.

In a skillet, add half the oil. Fry the chicken until golden.

Transfer the chicken to a plate.

Add the butter on the skillet.

Add the capers, lime juice and seasoning.

Add garlic powder and rosemary.

Return the chicken to the skillet. Cook for 5 minutes.

Add to a serving plate. Top with arugula.

Place the potatoes on a baking sheet.

Add seasoning and some oil. Roast for 10 minutes. Flip and roast for another 8 minutes.

Serve the chicken and parsley with the potatoes.

25. Chicken Piccata with Mashed Potatoes

The mashed potatoes in this recipe are very flavorful with butter, chives, and oregano. The chicken piccata complements the mashed potatoes perfectly.

Preparation Time: 5 minutes

Cooking Time: 30 minutes

Serves: 4

Ingredients:

- 4 large potatoes
- 1/2 cup butter for mashed potatoes
- 4 tbsp butter
- 1 lime, sliced
- 2 tbsp lime juice
- 2 tbsp chives, minced
- 1 tbsp parsley, minced
- 1 tbsp oil
- 4 chicken breasts
- 1 can (4 oz) capers, in brine
- 1 tsp smoked paprika
- 1/2 tsp ginger powder
- 4 tbsp flour
- 1 tsp garlic powder
- Black pepper to taste
- Salt to taste
- 1 tsp oregano

Instructions:

Boil the potatoes until they are tender.

Remove the skin and mash them finely.

Add the 1/2 cup of butter, seasoning, chives and oregano.

Mash until it is silky. Keep aside.

Coat the chicken pieces in seasoning, garlic and flour.

In a large pan, add the oil and fry the chicken until golden.

Transfer the chicken onto a plate.

In the same pan, melt the butter over medium heat.

Add the lime slices, lime juice, seasoning, ginger and paprika.

Cook for 1 minute. Add the capers and cook for 2 minutes.

Add the chicken and cook for 5 minutes. Serve the chicken with mashed potatoes.

Add parsley on top.

26. Chicken Piccata with Spaghetti

The white chicken piccata on top of a spaghetti is the kind of comfort food you want during a lazy day.

Preparation Time: 5 minutes

Cooking Time: 20 minutes

Serves: 1

Ingredients:

- 1 cup spaghetti
- 1 chicken breast
- 1/3 lime, sliced
- 1 tsp lime juice
- 2 tbsp parsley, minced
- 1/4 can (1 oz) capers, in brine
- 1 tsp oregano
- 1/2 tsp white pepper
- Salt to taste
- 1 tsp butter

Instructions:

Coat the chicken in salt, white pepper and lime juice.

In a pan, melt the butter.

Add the chicken and capers. Add lime juice.

Cook for 5 minutes. Take off the heat.

Boil the spaghetti in salted water.

Drain and add to a serving bowl. Top with chicken.

Add parsley and lime slices on top. Sprinkle some oregano on top.

27. Creamy Chicken Piccata Soup

The creaminess of this soup is to die for. The chicken pieces, on the other hand, are a winner!

Preparation Time: 10 minutes

Cooking Time: 30 minutes

Serves: 4

Ingredients:

- 4 chicken thighs
- 1 cup potatoes
- 1 cup cheddar cheese, grated
- 4 tbsp breadcrumbs
- 2 cups milk
- 1 can (4 oz) capers, in brine
- 2 tbsp chives, minced
- 2 tbsp parsley, minced
- 1/2 tsp ginger paste
- 1/2 tsp garlic powder
- 1 tsp smoked paprika
- Salt and pepper
- 1 tbsp olive oil

Instructions:

Coat the chicken thighs in breadcrumbs, salt, pepper, and garlic powder.

In a skillet, add the olive oil.

Fry the chicken pieces until golden brown.

In a pot, add the potatoes with 1 cup of water.

Cook until tender. Use a hand blender and blend until smooth.

Add the milk, salt, pepper, paprika, ginger, and cook for 8 minutes.

Add capers, chicken, and cheese.

Add chives and parsley.

Cook for 8 minutes. Serve hot.

28. Chicken Piccata Penne Pasta

Who does not love pasta? When you add chicken piccata to it, it becomes irresistible.

Preparation Time: 5 minutes

Cooking Time: 20 minutes

Serves: 4

Ingredients:

- 2 cups penne pasta
- 3 chicken breasts
- 3 tbsp flour
- 2 tbsp butter
- 1 tbsp oil
- 1 tbsp parsley, chopped
- 2 shallots, chopped
- 1/4 cup minced garlic
- 1/2 tsp paprika
- Salt and white pepper

Instructions:

Coat the chicken pieces in flour, salt, white pepper.

In a pan, add the oil.

Fry the chicken until golden brown.

Transfer to a plate.

Cut it into small pieces.

Boil the pasta in water for 6 minutes.

Drain it. In a large pan, melt the butter.

Fry the garlic and shallot for 3 minutes.

Add the chicken, pasta, paprika, and cook for 6 minutes.

Add the parsley and serve.

29. Chicken Piccata Veg Soup

This chicken piccata soup with noodles and bell pepper is quite delightful.

Preparation Time: 5 minutes

Cooking Time: 20 minutes

Serves: 4

Ingredients:

- 1 red bell pepper, julienne
- 1 yellow bell pepper, julienne
- 1 cup noodles
- 1 lime, sliced
- 1 tbsp lime juice
- 2 tbsp lemongrass, chopped
- 2 chicken breasts, cut into small pieces
- 2 cups chicken broth
- 1 tsp smoked paprika
- 1 tbsp parsley, minced
- 1 tsp garlic powder
- 1 tbsp oil
- Salt and pepper to taste

Instructions:

Coat the chicken pieces in garlic, salt and pepper.

In a pan, add the oil. Fry the chicken pieces for 4 minutes.

In a large pot, add the chicken broth with lemongrass, salt, pepper and paprika.

Cook for 5 minutes.

Add noodles, cooked chicken, bell peppers and cook for 6 minutes.

Add the parsley, lime juice and lime slices and then cook for 1 minute.

Serve hot.

30. Artichoke Spinach Chicken Piccata

The combination of artichoke and spinach with chicken piccata is very healthy.

Preparation Time: 10 minutes

Cooking Time: 30 minutes

Serves: 6

Ingredients:

- 1 can artichoke hearts, drained
- 1 cup spinach
- 6 chicken thighs, boneless
- 4 tbsp butter
- 2 tbsp lime juice
- 1/2 can (2 oz) capers, in brine
- 4 tbsp flour
- 1 tsp oregano
- 1/3 tsp paprika
- 1 tsp garlic powder
- Salt and pepper

Instructions:

Coat the chicken thighs in flour, salt, garlic.

In a pan, add 1 tbsp butter.

Fry the chicken thighs until golden brown.

Transfer the chicken thighs on a plate.

In a large pan, melt the remaining butter.

Add artichoke hearts and toss for 2 minutes.

Add capers, lime juice, seasoning, oregano and paprika.

Cook for 2 minutes. Return the chicken.

Add the spinach. Cook for 5 minutes. Serve.

Conclusion

Who knew chicken piccata had so wide varieties? With the recipes from the book, you will never be bored with chicken piccata recipes. You can try a different version of chicken piccata every week, thanks to this book.

You will find the traditional way of cooking chicken piccata and then there comes the fusion, where you get to mix and combine different types of recipes together.

For example, we all love pasta and having chicken piccata flavored with pasta is a killer combination for any pasta lover.

For me, I love the simple way of cooking chicken piccata that is ready in 15 minutes. I do enjoy the complex recipes occasionally, but quick recipes are always my number one go-to! Which one do you like the most?

Author's Afterthoughts

Lately, I've been trying to come up with ideas for my new cookbooks, but I thought that your ideas could be a huge help. Sure, I develop the recipes, but you're the one who makes them at home and brings them into your life! As a result, I want my recipes to be filled with flavors and ingredients that you keep in your kitchen at all times, ready to surprise unexpected guests.

I know a lot of my books are centered around treats and dishes for special occasions, but what else would you like to see from me? I'm still working on outlines, so now's the time to share your input with me. Do you think they are easy enough to follow along? Are the ingredients generally easy to find in your local supermarket? Would you like to see more recipes oriented toward a certain cuisine?

The only reason I have this amazing job and cook delicious food for a living is because of you, so now it's my turn to say thanks and contribute to your menus by preparing a cookbook worthy of your kitchen.

Thanks a bunch, xxx

Jayden Dixon

About the Author

How Jayden stumbled into the kitchen after spending much of her life working in oil rigs around the world is something she's not quite able to herself, but everyone is equally excited that she did! Working in some of the most remote locations on earth, literally cut off from civilization, she admits cooking (or eating) wasn't her favorite thing to do. Ingredients were pretty limited, as were food storage options with many people on the platform.

Whenever she video called friends and family, she liked to joke that canned tuna was her favorite meal! Fortunately, when her job permanently relocated her to actual land, she fell in love with supermarkets. Her mom says that's the only place Jayden went to and spent hours in for the first three months. Funnily enough, Jayden also happened to meet her husband, Max, at the supermarket, right by the canned goods aisle!

Neither of them knew how to cook, but they kept at it until they became amateur cooks capable of exceptional dishes. Word of mouth spread little by little, and locals started asking the pair to cater to their events. Eventually, the cooking began to eat up too much of their schedules, and they decided to quit their jobs and start their catering business in Milwaukee, Wisconsin. Six years later, Jayden and Max run the biggest catering service in Wisconsin. They have 3 lovely kids and 5 fluffy cats.